Sourdough Bread Made Easy

John Carroll

Table of Contents

1: INTRODUCTION

Sourdough bread is produced from three simple ingredients: flour, water and salt. It does not require the addition of commercial yeast as the sourdough process forms its own naturally occurring yeast in the sourdough culture. This has two consequences: first the bread is pure and natural and second, due to the acidity of the sourdough culture, the bread has a distinctive sour dough taste.

Once people have tasted proper sourdough bread there is often no going back to commercial yeast-raised bread. However, because of the time it takes to make, it is more expensive in shops than commercially-produced yeast bread and consequently not so widely available. This has led to a growing number of people opting to produce their own sourdough bread. Although it takes a bit more time overall, there is very little extra work involved than in baking ordinary yeast bread, so if planned properly it can require little or no additional effort.

I began making my own bread a few years back, first using a bread machine and then by hand. I produced wholemeal and mixed grain bread along with French baguettes and pizzas. All produced using dried yeast with good results but I always had a yearning to try sourdough bread. Two things put me off: the many conflicting methods and the need to produce a sourdough starter before being able to make sourdough bread. It all sounded a bit tricky and time consuming but I was wrong, it turned out to be simplicity itself!

But before I discovered that I read a lot of books and on-line reference material, which only made matters worse. Everyone had their own methods and recipes and they then confused the issue by talking about hydration and all sorts of other technical jargon. Which brings me to the purpose of this book. My background is project management consultancy and over the past fifteen or so years I have written a number of technical guides for the In Easy Steps series. The whole purpose of that series is to make complicated subjects easy to follow and that, I realized, was what was missing from sourdough bread making, hence in this book I have tried to keep everything as simple and easy to follow as possible.

With that in mind the chapters in this book are quite short and each one focuses on a single topic, which is then covered in simple steps, with plenty of illustrations.

Chapter 2 consists of a very brief history of sourdough bread and some of the technicalities behind it if you are interested in them, but please feel free to skip it if not.

When I finally got started on producing sourdough bread, I tried out all the various methods and recipes, with varying degrees of success, until I finally hit on a method that works perfectly every time. That method not only guarantees success, it is simplicity itself. However it does require time so what if you need to make some bread in a hurry?

There are two options: cheat and add some dried yeast to the sourdough bread mix to give it a helping hand; or use baking soda to make soda bread instead, it makes a nice change. I have included a recipe for quick sourdough bread (with the addition of dried yeast) which doesn't taste bad but is not as good as the real thing. My own preferred solution is to make soda bread. It not only tastes great but it takes less than an hour from start to finish. So I have also included a basic soda bread recipe as well.

The first part of the book covers the sourdough methods, processes, tools and techniques. The second part of the book features a series of recipes using different methods and ingredients, followed by an ingredient calculator in both metric and imperial to allow you to pick the size of loaf you want to make and a series of references and links to other sourdough bread resources and suppliers.

Backing this book up I also publish a blog called Sourdough Adventures (sourdougheasy.blogspot.co.uk) where I am always happy to receive feedback and questions.

So happy reading and, more importantly, happy sourdough bread making.

2: BRIEF HISTORY

In order to have the correct texture, bread dough needs to leaven (rise and become aerated). Commercial bakers use baker's yeast and home bakers typically use dried yeast. While this can produce a good texture (crumb) it can often be a little lacking in flavor. Sourdough bread on the other hand does not require the addition of any other yeast and it also has a great flavor.

Sourdough bread has been around for a long time and is thought to have originated in ancient Egypt around 1500 BC. In fact sourdough was the normal way of leavening bread until the middle ages when it started being replaced by yeast from the brewing process. Later still came the development of baker's yeast and you might say it all went downhill from there!

Sourdough was the main bread made during the California Gold Rush, and it still remains a part of the culture of San Francisco today. The bread became so common that "sourdough" became a general nickname for the gold prospectors. Although sourdough bread was superseded in commercial bakeries in the 20th century, it has undergone a revival among artisan bakers in recent years.

All sourdough bread starts with a sourdough culture or starter. Sourdough starters are used all over the world and they are always handled in a similar way. The baker never uses all of the starter. Each time they use some of the starter to make a loaf or batch of bread, the remainder is refreshed with flour and water and saved for the next baking session. In this way the starter is maintained and effectively lasts forever. There are some bakers I have heard of that are still using starters first produced by their great-grandparents or even earlier generations.

A sourdough starter is a mixture of wild yeast and lactobacillus bacteria, living in a mixture of flour and water. The yeast and lactobacillus bacteria form a symbiosis that is interesting and makes the culture quite stable. The yeast produces the carbon dioxide gas that leavens or aerates the dough, while the lactobacillus makes the culture acidic. The acidity also acts as an antibiotic, keeping stray bacteria and yeast out. Few yeast strains can survive in a sourdough culture but those that can survive the acidity produced by the lactobacillus will thrive. The lactobacillus also eat the dead yeast cells, which helps keep the culture from getting nasty. When compared to breads made with baker's yeast, the sourdough starter produces a mildly sour taste because of the lactic acid produced by the lactobacilli. This is what gives sourdough bread its distinct taste.

Incidentally, bread made from rye flour, is nearly always leavened with sourdough or baking soda. Baker's yeast is not a good leavening agent for rye bread, as rye flour does not contain enough gluten for it to act on.

Anyway enough about history, let's look at the basic sourdough process, it probably hasn't changed since the ancient Egyptians developed it and it consists of just four steps:

Step 1: produce the sourdough starter

Step 2: mix the ingredients to form the dough

Step 3: knead the dough and leave it to prove

Step 4: bake the bread and leave it to cool

The final three steps are exactly the same as baking with baker's yeast, the only difference is that the proving time is much longer (typically six to twelve hours rather than two hours). The longer proving time is because the natural yeast in the sourdough takes longer to prove than commercial baker's yeast but that's what gives it such a great taste.

The next four chapters will expand on each of the four steps above, in a series of simple and easy steps (with plenty of illustrations), starting with producing the sourdough starter.

3: SOURDOUGH STARTER

The preparation of sourdough begins with a pre-ferment, usually called the starter (but also known as the leaven or mother), and made of flour and water. The purpose of the starter is to produce a vigorous sourdough culture and to develop the flavor of the bread. In practice the ratio of water to flour in the starter (hydration) can be varied between something like a runny batter to a fairly stiff dough.

If you happen to know a friendly artisan baker they may be prepared to give or sell you some of their sourdough starter. You can also order it on-line (see Links at the end of the book) but part of the fun of the sourdough process is to create your own starter and although it takes around a week, it couldn't be simpler.

Some recipes for starting a sourdough culture call for the use of grapes or other types of fruits or even vegetables in the theory that they have yeast on their skins. But, while this is true, the types of yeast on the skins aren't appropriate. They may help the culture to get started but in the end, the yeast on the skins of the fruit or vegetable matter will die off. These starters may also have some strange characteristics and I suggest you keep it pure and simple and use just flour and water, it's really all you need. And, like all living things, a sourdough culture needs to be fed from time to time, and what it is fed on is again simply flour and water.

Getting Started

The first thing you will need is a container to keep your starter culture in, a click-lock plastic jar, a stone jar or a glass Kilner-type jar are all ideal, anywhere between half a litre (pint) and a litre (quart) but small enough to keep in your fridge when you are not using it. The only other two things you need are flour and water. The flour can be either rye flour or an unbleached, strong white bread flour or even a mixture of both but I would recommend starting with strong white bread flour initially unless you are only planning to make pure rye bread.

As it ferments over several days, the volume of the starter culture needs to be increased (refreshed) by the addition of more flour and water. As long as the starter culture is fed flour and water regularly it will remain active.

Day One

In your starter container, mix together a small cup of flour (about 30g/1oz) and the same amount of tepid water (around 20°C/68°F), cover it and leave at room temperature (again around 20°C/68°F) for 24 hours.

Flour, container, cup and water, ready to go.

Days Two to Six

Refresh or feed your starter by mixing in one small cup of flour and one small cup of tepid water and leave it at room temperature for another 24 hours. If your container is getting close to full, throw away part of the contents (or add it to your compost bin) before feeding it.

For the first few days, the mixture may seem a bit lifeless and might smell a bit strange. Don't worry about this as by day four or five, it should start bubbling and the smell will develop into something yeasty and slightly acidic.

Tip: If your starter is a bit lethargic (and it will take longer in a cooler room), repeat the refreshment for another day or two until it comes to life.

Once your starter is bubbling it is ready to use. You can use some of it straight away or keep it in the fridge until you are ready to use it.

Starter bubbling and ready to use

Caring for your Starter

Some people like to give their starter a name, they say you can't call yourself a proper sourdough nut if you don't, but in my humble opinion this is optional. Do get to know your starter though, they all have varying acidity, tastes, aromas and speeds at which they ferment. Most important of all, unless you are using it and feeding it every day, keep it in the fridge until you need it.

Then each time you use some of the starter, simply replace what you have used with an equivalent quantity of flour and water. When refreshing your starter, you could try experimenting with different ratios and total amounts of flour to water: a looser starter will ferment more quickly than a stiff one; refreshing more often or adding a large refreshment will dilute the taste and acidity. But for general ease of use just use the same volume of flour and water to keep things simple.

When you are not using the starter, just forget it. You may only bake bread once or twice a week and your starter can even be left untouched in the fridge for weeks at a time. The yeast and bacteria will decline over time but enough will live on in a dormant state. To revive it, just take it out of the fridge, bring it up to room temperature, give it a feed by adding flour and water and leave it at room temperature for a couple of hours until it's bubbling again.

You can also experiment with substituting rye flour for wheat in the starter and vice versa. Or you may choose to get a separate rye starter going. You can use a rye starter to make wheat bread as well as rye bread.

4: BASIC SOURDOUGH

There are many different recipes and methods for sourdough bread but let's start with the basics. This is a simple basic recipe for producing sourdough bread which uses the same process as making bread with commercial yeast. It will produce a quite acceptable loaf.

These quantities will produce a 660g (about a 1½lb) loaf (if you want to produce a different size loaf see the calculator at the back of the book).

Ingredients

Flour	350g	strong white bread flour
Water	175ml	preferably filtered water at room temperature
Starter	175ml	sourdough starter at room temperature
Salt	1 teaspoon	preferably sea salt

First put the flour and salt into a mixing bowl and mix them together.

Then put the water and sourdough starter into a measuring jug and mix them together.

Mixing

Now make a well in the centre of the mixing bowl and slowly add the water and sourdough starter stirring it until you have added all the liquid and have formed a solid ball of dough. Add a little more flour if it is too runny or a little more water if it is too dry. It should end up as a solid but slightly sticky ball of dough.

Dough in mixing bowl

Machines

If you have a mixing machine with a dough hook it can perform the basic dough mixing function perfectly well. It can also carry out the kneading of the dough for you, although the ten minutes spent kneading the dough is part of the joy of bread making for me (for as long as I am still able to do it).

Bread making machines on the other hand are a different proposition. While it may be possible, theoretically, to program them for the complete process of making sourdough bread, I doubt that the results would be satisfactory. If you do want to use a bread machine I suggest you just use it for the mixing and kneading, then carry on by hand.

5: KNEADING & PROVING

Once you have produced the dough in the mixing bowl, turn it out onto a lightly floured surface. You may find a plastic dough scraper useful for getting all the dough out as some tends to stick to the sides of the bowl.

Kneading the Dough

If the dough is very sticky add a little more flour, if it is too dry add a little more water, but err on the side of stickiness to begin with. As you knead the dough it will become less sticky.

First stretch the dough out into a long strand.

Then roll it back together into a rough ball.

Continue this process, stretching in a different direction each time.

After around 10 minutes the dough should feel smooth and satiny. You can test it by pinching the top of the ball and picking it up. The dough should stretch out thinly. This is referred to by some people as the 'window pane' test as it should, in theory, be thin enough to almost see through. If the dough is not smooth and satiny then knead it for a little longer.

Dough Proof

Now form the dough into a ball and put it into a lightly oiled bowl.

Cover the bowl with cling film and leave it to prove in a warm place for two to four hours until roughly doubled in size. If you live in a warm country the kitchen will probably be fine, if not a warm airing cupboard should be fine or put it in the oven with just the oven light on (which is what I do as I was told off for getting flour on the clothes in the airing cupboard).

You won't notice as much of a rise in the dough as you would with a yeasted bread which is why it will take longer. The warmer the temperature the quicker the rise, so the first time check it every hour and once it is roughly doubled in size you are ready for the next step.

Risen dough in bowl

Loaf Proof

Once the dough is roughly doubled in size, turn it out onto a lightly floured surface to knock it back and shape it.

Knocking back consists of punching the dough gently to get rid of the gas in it and rolling it back into a ball. It should be roughly back to its original size following this.

Shaping the dough consists of rolling it into the required shape for your baking sheet or bread tin. Then place the shaped dough on a baking sheet or in a bread tin and sprinkle the top with flour (see illustration overleaf).

Shaped dough on baking sheet

Cover with a clean tea towel and leave it to prove in a warm place for a further two to four hours until it is again roughly doubled in size again.

Risen dough on baking sheet

6: BAKING

Preheat the oven to 230°C (190°C fan), 450°F or gas mark 8 (but please do remember to remove the risen dough from the oven before turning it on if that is where you were proving it!).

Put a small amount (about 100ml) of cold water into a metal tray or small oven-proof dish and place in the bottom of the oven to create some steam. This encourages the bread to rise and helps develop a crisp crust.

Using a sharp bread knife, score the top of the risen loaf. This is referred to as the baker's signature and can be any pattern you like. The purpose is to allow the top of the crust to expand without splitting when it goes into the hot oven (called the oven spring).

Risen and slashed loaf in oven (with tray of water below)

Bake for 40-45 minutes or until a good golden crust has formed and the loaf sounds hollow when tapped on the base.

Note: baking time will vary from oven to oven, so be prepared to shorten or lengthen the baking time as required. When the loaf is perfect, make a note of the time and use that in future.

Turn the oven off and leave the loaf in the cooling oven, with the door slightly open (to get rid of any remaining steam) for a further 5 minutes.

Then remove the loaf from the oven and put it on a rack to cool for at least an hour. This is sometimes hard to do as the smell of the fresh baked bread is wonderful but it is better for the bread to let it cool down before cutting it.

Loaf cooling on rack

Once cooled, slice, spread with butter and enjoy.

7: TOOLS

At the simplest level, the basic tools you will need are a container for your starter, a mixing bowl, a spoon, a baking tray and oven gloves. You will also need to weigh and measure the ingredients but all of these should already be present in most kitchens. There are a number of other items that will help the process and enhance the end product. These are the tools that I use:

500g click-lock container for the starter:

I started out with one but quickly decided two would be better as it does get a bit mucky with bits of dried starter sticking to the sides. When it gets like this and I am ready to feed the starter, I simply add a cup of water, stir it up to mix it and transfer the mixture to the second container. I then add a cup of flour and mix it up again to complete the feeding process. Leave it for a couple of hours and return it to the fridge. Then wash the other container.

Scales for weighing the ingredients:

These are a bit ancient but they were a wedding present and I am rather fond of them.

Measuring jug and small cups:

The measuring jug is for measuring liquid ingredients (water and starter) and the small cups for feeding the starter with equal volumes of flour and water.

I started out using the cup on the left (an Americano coffee cup) but found I was producing too much starter, so I switched to the smaller espresso coffee cup on the right. You can probably deduce from this that I like coffee.

Mixing bowls:

The one on the left is a Judge stainless steel bowl that I use for mixing the dough. The one on the right is a 3 litre Pyrex glass mixing bowl I use as a cloche (see page 30), but it also doubles as a mixing bowl.

Spurtle:

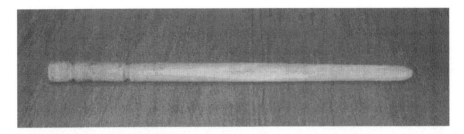

It is a traditional Scottish wooden porridge stirrer, which I find great for mixing dough. Alternatively you could use a wooden spoon or even your fingers for mixing the dough.

Plastic dough scrapers:

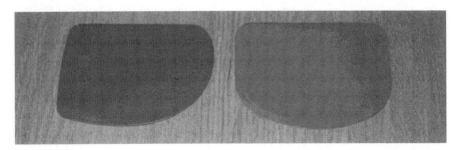

Plastic dough scrapers come in many shapes, sizes and colours. They are great for getting the last few bits of dough out of the mixing bowl (using the curved sides) and for getting dough of the work surface if it is too sticky (using the straight side). You can get metal dough scrapers but I prefer the plastic ones.

Baking tray:

This is a 39cm x 27cm non-stick baking tray but it works even better with the non-stick baking sheet (or parchment), cut to fit, inside it.

The alternative, if you want a regular loaf-shaped loaf is to use a non-stick bread tin.

Sharp bread knife:

For slashing the top of the dough as well as for slicing the finished product. But do keep it very sharp, if not it will pull and tear the dough rather than cutting it cleanly. Some people use razor blades for the job and the French even have special handles for holding them (called a Lame) but a sharp bread knife works fine and you can use it for slicing bread too!

Tip: if you slash the top of the dough with the blade at a 45° angle the bread will develop fine crusty ears, which are much prized, particularly in Pain au Lavain (page 40).

8: OTHER METHODS

There are many different methods for making sourdough bread and the following are some of the variations to the basic method:

Long First Rise

Some sourdough bakers employ a long first rise (sometimes with a long second rise). It does develop the sourdough flavour, but it also increases the overall time and there is another alternative (see sponge method later in this chapter). Make the dough and knead it as for the basic method. Place it in a lightly oiled bowl, cover with cling film and leave it to prove in a cool place for six to eight hours (or overnight), but do read the warning below. At the end of this time it should be roughly doubled in size. Knock the dough back, shape the loaf and carry on as for the basic method or long second rise.

Long Second Rise

This is really the classic sourdough approach. Make the dough, knead and prove as for the basic method (or long first rise). When it has roughly doubled in size, tip the dough onto a lightly floured work surface, knock it back and knead it briefly. Work the dough into the required shape, cover with a sheet of lightly oiled cling film and leave in a cool place for six to eight hours, until doubled in size (but see warning below) and then bake as normal.

Warning: depending on the ambient temperature the long first or second rise may take a lot less or a lot more time. If it is left too long or at too high a temperature the dough may collapse back on itself after rising. If you are fortunate enough to live in a warm climate and want to try a long rise, then see "refrigerate the dough" method on page 23.

Low Effort

This low-effort approach to kneading was developed by baking legend Dan Lepard and takes a bit longer (although most of the additional time is spent waiting so you can do other things). Make the dough as for the basic method (but leave out the salt) and leave it to sit in the mixing bowl for 30 minutes. Then add a teaspoonful of salt, mix the ingredients again for just 15 seconds and leave it for 15 minutes. Then mix again for 15 seconds and leave it for another 15 minutes. Finally mix again for 15 seconds and then leave the dough to prove (first rise) as for the basic method.

Single Rise

The basic reason for knocking back the proven dough is to remove large bubbles and get a more even crumb. But one of the delights of sourdough bread is an uneven crumb so simply don't bother with a second rise. The following method builds on this.

Stretch and Fold

This method combines kneading with a single rise. Make the dough as for the basic method but, instead of stretching and rolling, gently stretch the dough into a 20cm to 30cm square. Now fold one side in about one third of the way.

Stretched dough with one side folded in

Fold the other side in to overlap the first and form a long rectangle. Then fold in the two ends of the rectangle a third of the way to create a square. The aim is to trap air, so be gentle. Turn the dough over, smooth it into a rough ball and put it back in the bowl. Cover with cling film and leave it in a warm place for 20 minutes. Then repeat this stretching, folding and resting process twice more, notice how the dough gradually puffs up. After the third rest, gently form the dough into your final loaf shape then leave it for a final 40 to 60 minutes (until doubled in size) before baking as normal.

Sponge Method

Sponge refers to a preparatory mix of half of the flour with all of the water and starter. Prepare the sponge in a mixing bowl, cover with cling film and leave to prove in a cool place for six to eight hours. Then add the remaining flour and salt and continue as usual. This is effectively a long first raise.

Sponge after proving

Refrigerate the Dough

One of the problems with using the long second proof is the danger of the dough rising too much and then collapsing back on itself. A very sad sight to see. It is a particular problem in warmer climates but this next method overcomes that risk.

It is similar to a long second proof but by putting the dough in the fridge overnight (or all day) it slows the rise down. Then bring the dough out of the fridge and allow it to come up to room temperature for an hour or so to finish rising and bake as normal. Alternatively take the dough straight out of the fridge and follow the bake from cold method (below).

Bake from Cold

Instead of pre-heating the oven, bake from cold. Once the dough is nearly doubled in size but not fully risen (which reduces the rise time by about an hour) put it into a cold oven and bake as usual but add the time it takes the oven to get up to heat to the bake time. In my oven, which is an electric fan oven, this only takes five minutes, but all ovens vary so time it exactly the first time and then simply add the time to the baking time.

Trying the Methods

Please do try out the various methods as one or more may be ideal for you. Having worked my way through each of the methods and combinations of them I have found the one combination that works every time and produces great bread. This is the combination that works for me:

Sponge Method (I leave it to prove overnight in the cool kitchen).

Single Rise in a warm place (the sponge method is effectively the first rise so there is no need for two more).

Bake from Cold (which reduces the single rise time to around two and a half hours).

And that's it.

This combination of methods is set out in the following chapter (Better Sourdough).

Note: Using the sponge method does change the ratio of flour, water and starter, but the recipes reflect this and there are separate sections for the two methods in the Calculator at the back of the book.

Tip: Although I don't use it for sourdough bread, I do use the stretch and fold technique when making sourdough baguettes (see page 46).

9: BETTER SOURDOUGH

Having worked my way through every combination of the variations in the previous chapter, I finally arrived at the one method that works for me every time and produces really good bread. I usually bake in the morning so the following method starts in the evening, but if you want to bake in the evening just start in the morning, the steps are the same in either case.

Method

Unless otherwise stated, all these recipes will produce a 660g loaf (about 1½ pounds), using a bread tin or baking tray. If you want to produce a different size loaf see the calculator at the back of the book.

Ingredients

Flour	400g	strong white bread flour
Water	220ml	preferably filtered water at room temperature
Starter	100ml	sourdough starter at room temperature
Salt	1 teaspoon	preferably sea salt

Sponge Proof

Get the sourdough starter out of the fridge and bring it up to room temperature for about 2 hours. Make the sponge by mixing the sourdough starter, water and half the flour but not the salt and leave it in the mixing bowl covered with cling-film overnight in a cool place.

Feed the starter with enough flour and water to replace the starter used, leave it at room temperature for 2 hours (it should be foaming and bubbling by then) and then return it to the fridge.

Loaf Proof

In the morning remove the cling film and the sponge should be fermenting (thick and bubbly):

Bubbling sponge

Add the other half of the flour and salt and mix well. Add more flour or water if necessary but keep the dough as sticky as possible.

Turn the dough out onto a lightly floured surface and knead until the dough is smooth and satiny (around 10 minutes).

Shape the dough and put it in a bread tin or on a baking sheet, dust with flour, cover with a tea towel and proof in a warm place for two to three hours until nearly doubled in size. I proof it in the oven with the oven light on.

Bake

Slash the top of the loaf with a sharp bread knife and put it in on a low shelf in the oven. Put 100ml of water into a metal tray or ovenproof dish in the bottom of the oven (to create steam) and set the oven to 230°C (190°C fan), 450°F or gas mark 8. Bake for 40 to 45 minutes once the oven has got up to temperature or until the crust is golden, turn the oven off and leave the bread in the cooling oven, with the door slightly open for another 5 minutes. Then turn the loaf out onto a rack to cool for at least an hour before slicing.

Baked loaf cooling

Getting a Crisp Crust

If you check out some baking web sites and blogs (see links at the end of the book), you will find that one of the biggest issues is about getting a nice crisp crust on your bread. The answer is providing steam in the oven during the early part of baking. Professional bakers use sealed ovens that have steam pipes to provide steam just when it is needed. Unfortunately most domestic ovens are not sealed and have no provision for creating steam.

The simple answer is to put some cold water (or even ice cubes) in a hot dish in the bottom of the oven as set out in this recipe. Too little water will not produce enough steam and too much will stop the crust crisping. So measure it accurately and if there is any water left in the dish half way through the bake take it out and reduce the amount of water the next time.

Another option is to get a water spray/atomizer and squirt water into the oven several times during the early stages of baking. Some people swear by this technique but it does mean keeping opening the oven door, which can also impact on the crust.

The best method is to enclose the loaf during the early part of the bake (as the dough itself gives off steam) using a covered casserole dish, metal Dutch oven or a cloche (baking dome). Then remove the lid part way through baking so that the crust crisps up. This is covered in the next section (Heading for Perfection).

Heading for Perfection

There are two further improvements that can be made to the better sourdough method and that is to use a banneton and cloche. As you can probably guess these are both French terms. A banneton is a proving basket (used instead of a bread tin to form the loaf) and a cloche is simply a cover that fits over the baking dish or sheet. A cloche will improve the rise of the bread by trapping the steam given off and produce a nicer crust, without the need for water in the oven.

The La Cloche baking dome (illustrated above) is currently the best on the market but it costs around £50 in the UK. I checked the same item for US prices and was amazed to discover that they are about the same in US dollars as we pay in UK pounds (it seems like we Brits are getting ripped off). But there is a much cheaper alternative. I use a bread baking dish with a three litre Pyrex mixing bowl (illustrated on page 30) at a total cost around £15 and you can even see what's happening to the dough inside it!

Bannetons come in different sizes, shapes (although most are round) and patterns so you should be able to find one for the size of loaf you want to bake. Simply shape the dough into a ball (or sausage if you are using a long banneton), put it in the floured banneton, sprinkle some flour on top, cover with a tea towel and proof in a warm place for two to three hours until nearly doubled in size.

Round cane banneton

Once the dough has risen, put the baking sheet or dish upside down on top of the banneton, invert the two and carefully lift off the banneton, leaving the dough on the baking sheet or dish as illustrated below:

Dough turned out of banneton

Cloche Use

To use the cloche simply place it over the dough (after slashing the top) so that it sits on the baking sheet or dish, put it in a cold oven and bake at 230°C (190°C fan), 450°F or gas mark 8 for 25 minutes after the oven comes up to temperature.

Cloche in position in the oven

Then carefully remove the cloche (take care, it will be very hot):

Loaf in oven after cloche removed

After 25 minutes (or when the loaf is a nice golden colour) turn the oven off and leave the loaf in the cooling oven, with the door slightly open for a further 5 minutes. Then take the loaf out of the oven and put it onto a cooling rack for at least an hour before slicing.

Baked loaf cooling

So here is the better sourdough bread method using a banneton and cloche for the best sourdough bread:

Best Sourdough Bread

Flour	400g	strong white bread flour
Water	220ml	preferably filtered water at room temperature
Starter	100ml	sourdough starter at room temperature
Salt	1 teaspoon	preferably sea salt

Sponge Proof

In the evening, get the sourdough starter out of the fridge and bring it up to room temperature for about 2 hours (it should foam and bubble). Make the sponge by mixing the sourdough starter, water and half the flour but not the salt and leave in a bowl covered with cling-film overnight.

Feed the starter with enough flour and water to replace the starter used, leave it at room temperature for 2 hours and then return it to the fridge.

Loaf Proof

In the morning the sponge should be fermenting (thick and bubbly). Add the other half of the flour and salt and mix well. Add more flour or water if necessary but keep the dough as sticky as possible.

Turn the dough out onto a lightly floured surface and knead until the dough is smooth and satiny (around 10 minutes).

Shape the dough for the floured banneton, sprinkle flour on top, cover with a tea towel and prove in a warm place for two to three hours until nearly doubled in size.

Bake

Invert the dough onto the baking dish, slash the top, cover with the cloche, put into a cold oven and bake at 230°C (190°C fan), 450°F or gas mark 8 for 25 minutes once the oven has come up to temperature.

Remove the cloche and bake for another 25 minutes until golden. Turn the oven off and leave the bread in the cooling oven, with the oven door slightly open, for another 5 minutes, then turn the loaf out onto a rack to cool for at least an hour.

Then slice, spread with butter and enjoy.

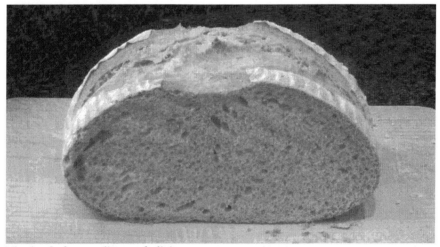

The loaf after cooling and slicing

10: TROUBLESHOOTING

We all have the occasional problem, particularly in the early days of baking sourdough bread. These are some of the more common ones:

Bread Fails to Rise

Or rises very slowly. There are two common causes for this: (a) too much salt (in addition to flavouring, the salt also acts as a yeast inhibitor, which slows down the rise) try using a little less salt; (b) the ambient temperature is too cold, try putting the dough somewhere warmer for proving. I use the oven with just the electric pilot light on.

Dough Collapses

This is the opposite of the first problem, and usually happens because the dough has risen too quickly. The most common causes are also the opposite: (a) you forgot to add the salt or didn't add enough, make sure you add the amount in the recipe or increase it slightly; (b) the ambient temperature is too warm, either shorten the proving time or prove in the fridge to start with.

Poor Crust

Ideally we want a nice crisp, golden crust. The most common causes of a soft crust are: not baked long enough or at too low a temperature (all ovens are different so try increasing the bake time or increasing the temperature); not enough steam in the early stage of baking or too much steam later (see getting a crisp crust on page 27). The other possibility is that the loaf has become damp after baking, typically by putting the bread in a sealed container before it has cooled down completely. Wait at least four hours after baking.

Not Fully Baked

Also known as 'soggy bottom'. The loaf looks fine when you take it out of the oven but when it cools down the bottom is soggy and not fully cooked. The answer is to check the loaf when you think it is baked by taking it out of the oven and tapping it on the bottom. The bottom should be tight and sound hollow when tapped. If not put it back in the oven for another fine minutes and try again. When it sounds right, turn the oven off and put the loaf back in the cooling oven, with the door slightly open for a further five minutes.

Dough Too Sticky

While the dough will become less sticky as it is worked, if it is too sticky it will be very difficult to handle. Just add a small amount of flour at a time until it becomes easier to handle, but try to keep the dough slightly on the sticky side to start with.

Dough Too Dry

If the dough won't stick together, it's the exact opposite of the sticky dough problem. Just add a little more water, but be very sparing or you will just flip to the previous problem. A little at a time is the rule for both problems.

Dough Spreads Out

If the dough spreads out on the baking tray during proving it is probably too wet. Try making it a little dryer or use a proving basket.

Bread Sticks to Baking Tray

Sprinkle a little more flour on the baking tray or dish (or on top of the dough before inverting if using a banneton).

Inactive Starter

If the starter becomes inactive after a long period of storage, get it out of the fridge, scrape off any mold and pour off any liquid (hooch) from the top. Then give it a good feed, leave it a day at room temperature, feed it again (discarding some of the starter if necessary) and repeat the process until it becomes active again.

If any of the above do not solve the problem, or if you experience any other problems please let me know via my Sourdough Adventures blog (at sourdougheasy.blogspot.co.uk) and I'll do what I can to help.

RECIPES

The first three recipes are summaries of the three recipes already set out in the first part of the book. The others are a classic sourdough recipe and some other variations you might like to try. As a general rule of thumb you can change the mixture of flour in any of the recipes, using strong white, whole meal, rye and any other types of flour (except self-raising, which contains baking soda). I have included some examples of this. Keep the total weight of flour the same just try different quantities of the different types.

Basic Sourdough
Better Sourdough
Best Sourdough
Classic Sourdough
Pain au Levain
Rustic Sourdough
Light Rye Sourdough
Light Wholemeal Sourdough
Sourdough Baguettes
Multi Grain Sourdough
Sourdough Pizza
Sourdough Bagels
Quick Sourdough
Soda Bread

Basic Sourdough

This is a simple recipe for producing sourdough bread using a double rise and it will produce a quite acceptable loaf. These quantities will produce a 660g (about a 1½lb) loaf (if you want to produce a different size loaf see the calculator at the end of the book).

Ingredients

Flour	350g	strong white bread flour
Water	175ml	preferably filtered water at room temperature
Starter	175ml	sourdough starter at room temperature
Salt	1 teaspoon	preferably sea salt

Method

Mix the starter and water in a measuring jug and mix the flour and salt in a large mixing bowl. Slowly add the water and sourdough starter to the flour and salt, stirring it until you have added all the liquid and have formed a solid ball of dough. Add a little more flour if it is too runny or a little more water if it is too dry. It should end up as a solid but slightly sticky ball of dough.

Transfer the dough to a lightly floured surface and knead until smooth and easy to handle (around 10 minutes) and form it into a smooth ball.

Return the dough to the mixing bowl, cover with cling film and leave to prove in a warm place for two to four hours until doubled in size.

Put the dough back on a floured surface, knock the dough back, shape the loaf, sprinkle with flour, cover with a tea towel and leave it to prove again in a warm place for two to four hours until doubled in size.

Slash the top of the loaf with a sharp bread knife and put it in on a low shelf in the oven. Put 100ml of water into an ovenproof dish in the bottom of the oven (to create steam) and set the oven to 230°C (190°C fan), 450°F or gas mark 8. Bake for 40 to 45 minutes once the oven has got up to temperature or until the crust is golden. Then turn the oven off and leave the bread in the cooling oven, with the door slightly open, for another 5 minutes, then turn the loaf out onto a rack to cool for at least an hour.

Tip: For a single raise just finish kneading the dough, then move onto shaping the loaf.

Better Sourdough

This method uses a sponge in place of the first rise and bake from cold for a shorter second rise. It produces really good bread consistently. I usually bake in the morning so the following method starts in the evening, but if you want to bake in the evening just start in the morning.

Ingredients

Flour	400g	strong white bread flour
Water	220ml	preferably filtered water at room temperature
Starter	100ml	sourdough starter at room temperature
Salt	1 teaspoon	preferably sea salt

Method

In the evening, get the sourdough starter out of the fridge and bring it up to room temperature for about 2 hours (it should foam and bubble). Make the sponge by mixing the sourdough starter, water and half the flour but not the salt and leave in a bowl covered with cling-film overnight.

Feed the starter with enough flour and water to replace the starter used, leave it at room temperature for 2 hours and then return it to the fridge.

In the morning the sponge should be fermenting (thick and bubbly). Add the other half of the flour and salt and mix well. Add more flour or water if necessary but keep the dough as sticky as possible.

Turn the dough out onto a lightly floured surface and knead until the dough is smooth and satiny (around 10 minutes).

Shape the dough and put it in a bread tin or on a baking sheet, dust with flour, cover with a tea towel and proof in a warm place for two to three hours until nearly doubled in size. I proof it in the oven with the oven light on.

Slash the top of the loaf with a sharp bread knife and put it in on a low shelf in the oven. Put 100ml of water into an ovenproof dish in the bottom of the oven (to create steam) and set the oven to 230°C (190°C fan), 450°F or gas mark 8. Bake for 40 to 45 minutes once the oven has got up to temperature or until the crust is golden, turn the oven off and leave the bread in the cooling oven, with the door slightly open, for another 5 minutes, then turn the loaf out onto a rack to cool for at least an hour.

Best Sourdough

This is the better sourdough method, using a banneton and cloche, and produces a really excellent sourdough loaf.

Ingredients

Flour	400g	strong white bread flour
Water	220ml	preferably filtered water at room temperature
Starter	100ml	sourdough starter at room temperature
Salt	1 teaspoon	preferably sea salt

Method

In the evening, get the sourdough starter out of the fridge and bring it up to room temperature for about 2 hours (it should foam and bubble). Make the sponge by mixing the sourdough starter, water and half the flour but not the salt and leave in a bowl covered with cling-film overnight.

Feed the starter with enough flour and water to replace the starter used, leave it at room temperature for 2 hours and then return it to the fridge.

In the morning the sponge should be fermenting (thick and bubbly). Add the other half of the flour and salt and mix well. Add more flour or water if necessary but keep the dough as sticky as possible.

Turn the dough out onto a lightly floured surface and knead until the dough is smooth and satiny (around 10 minutes).

Shape the dough into a ball and put it in the floured banneton, sprinkle flour on top, cover with a tea towel and proof in a warm place for two to three hours until nearly doubled in size.

Place the baking dish upside down on top of the banneton and invert the baking dish and banneton. Carefully lift off the banneton leaving the dough on the baking dish, slash the top, cover with the cloche, put into a cold oven and bake at 230°C (190°C fan), 450°F or gas mark 8 for 25 minutes once the oven has come up to temperature.

Remove the cloche and bake for another 25 minutes until golden. Turn the oven off and leave the bread in the cooling oven, with the door slightly open, for another 5 minutes, then turn the loaf out onto a rack to cool.

Classic Sourdough

By way of comparison to the preceding methods, this is a classic sourdough recipe from the BBC. In addition to the other ingredients it also uses olive oil to stop the dough sticking to things during kneading (which, interestingly, is neither classic nor traditional) but you might like to try it.

Ingredients

Flour   375g strong white flour, plus extra for dusting
Water   130-175ml tepid water
Starter 250g
Salt   7.5g
Olive oil for kneading

Method

Combine the flour, starter and salt in a large mixing bowl. Add the water, a little at a time, and mix with your hands to make a soft dough (you may not need all of the water).

Coat a chopping board or work surface with olive oil, then tip the dough onto it and knead the dough for 10 to 15 minutes, or until the dough is smooth and elastic.

Tip the dough into a lightly oiled bowl and cover with cling film. Leave to rise in a warm place for five hours, or until at least doubled in size.

Turn the dough out onto an oiled surface and knead it again until it's smooth, knocking the air out. Roll into a ball and dust with flour.

Tip the dough into a well-floured round banneton or proving basket and leave to rise for 4-8 hours.

Put a tray half filled with water on the bottom oven shelf and preheat the oven to 220°C/425°F/Gas 7.

Gently tip the risen dough onto a lined baking tray. Bake the loaf for 30 minutes at this heat, then reduce the heat to 200°C/400°F/Gas 6 and bake for a further 15-20 minutes. Cool on a cooling rack.

Tip: you can use the oiled kneading surface with any other recipes.

Pain au Levain

The classic French sourdough bread, typically made with a mixture of white and wholemeal or white and rye flour, takes from four to seven days to produce. However, we can use the better sourdough method to make a pretty good likeness of the classic small bâtard. The term bâtard (literally bastard) probably refers to the fact that these small loaves used the left over bits of dough from making larger loaves.

Ingredients

Flour	175g	strong white bread flour
	25g	rye or wholemeal flour
Water	110ml	preferably filtered water at room temperature
Starter	50ml	sourdough starter at room temperature
Salt	½ teaspoon	preferably sea salt

Method

In the evening, get the sourdough starter out of the fridge and bring it up to room temperature for about 2 hours (it should foam and bubble). Make the sponge by mixing the sourdough starter, water and half the flour but not the salt and leave in a bowl covered with cling-film overnight in a cool place.

In the morning the sponge should be fermenting (thick and bubbly). Add the other half of the flour and salt and mix well. Add more flour or water if necessary but keep the dough fairly firm. Turn the dough out onto a lightly floured surface and knead until the dough is smooth and satiny (around 10 minutes).

Shape the dough into a round ball, flatten the ball into a disc and then roll it up into a bâtard shape (shorter and stubbier than a baguette):

Dough bâtard

Create an oval proving basket (I used an oval Pyrex dish with a tea towel inside it) dust with flour, place the dough in the proving basket, dust the top with flour, cover with the tea towel and prove in a warm place for around two hours until nearly doubled in size.

Once risen, transfer the dough gently onto a baking tray

Dust the top lightly with flour, slash the top of the loaf along the length with a sharp bread knife at an angle of 45° and put the baking sheet on a middle shelf in the oven.

Put 100ml of water into an baking dish in the bottom of the oven (to create steam) and set the oven to 230°C (190°C fan), 450°F or gas mark 8. Bake for 35 to 40 minutes once the oven has got up to temperature or until the crust is golden, turn the oven off and leave the bread in the cooling oven, with the door slightly open for another 5 minutes:

Then turn out onto a rack to cool for at least an hour:

Tip: you can also use the best sourdough method by covering the dough with a cloche (the oval Pyrex dish would be fine) for the first half of the baking time instead of putting water in the oven to create steam.

Tip: the ingredients to make one bâtard are exactly half of the better/best sourdough recipe, so to make two bâtards just use the standard ingredients and halve the dough before shaping.

Rustic Sourdough

The Pain au Levain method gives the bread a nice "rustic" look and taste through the addition of a small quantity of wholemeal flour. So this recipe is a combination of the Better or Best Sourdough method with the Pain au Levain ingredients.

Ingredients

Flour	350g	strong white bread flour
	50g	wholemeal flour
Water	220ml	preferably filtered water at room temperature
Starter	100ml	sourdough starter at room temperature
Salt	1 teaspoon	preferably sea salt

Method

Make the sponge with 200g of strong white bread flour, 220ml of water and 100ml of starter.

In the morning add 50g of wholemeal flour, 150g of strong white bread flour and teaspoon of salt and proceed as for the Better Sourdough method on page 37 or the Best Sourdough method on page 38.

Light Rye Sourdough

For a stronger rye flavor but still keeping a nice light, open texture, this recipe can be used with the Better Sourdough method or Best Sourdough method (if you are using a banneton and cloche).

Ingredients

Flour	200g	rye bread flour
	200g	strong white bread flour
Water	220ml	preferably filtered water at room temperature
Starter	100ml	sourdough starter at room temperature
Salt	1 teaspoon	preferably sea salt

Method

Make the sponge with half of the rye and strong white bread flour, 220ml of water and 100ml of starter.

In the morning add the rest of the rye and strong white bread flour and a teaspoon of salt and proceed as for the Better Sourdough method on page 37 or the Best Sourdough method on page 38.

Light Wholemeal Sourdough

Pure wholemeal sourdough bread requires a longer rise time than white sourdough bread and has a heavier crumb. Mixing the wholemeal flour with strong white bread flour gives a better crumb and also means you can follow the Better Sourdough method or Best Sourdough method if you are using a banneton and cloche.

Ingredients

Flour	200g	wholemeal bread flour
	200g	strong white bread flour
Water	220ml	preferably filtered water at room temperature
Starter	100ml	sourdough starter at room temperature
Salt	1 teaspoon	preferably sea salt

Method

Make the sponge with 200g of strong white bread flour, 220ml of water and 100ml of starter.

In the morning add 200g of wholemeal flour and a teaspoon of salt and proceed as for the Better Sourdough method on page 37 or the Best Sourdough method on page 38.

Sourdough Baguettes

This recipe is based on the basic sourdough recipe but with a single rise and bake from cold to speed up the process. It produces two small baguettes (literally wands or battons), which are best baked on a baguette rack.

Ingredients

Flour	240g	strong white bread flour
Water	120ml	preferably filtered water at room temperature
Starter	120ml	sourdough starter at room temperature
Salt	¾ teaspoon	preferably sea salt

Method

Mix the starter and water in a measuring jug and mix the flour and salt in a large mixing bowl. Slowly add the water and sourdough starter to the flour and salt, stirring it until you have added all the liquid and have formed a solid ball of dough. Add a little more flour if it is too runny or a little more water if it is too dry. It should end up as a solid but slightly sticky ball of dough.

Transfer the dough to a lightly floured surface and knead until smooth and easy to handle (around 10 minutes) and form it into a smooth ball.

Divide the dough in two and then roll and shape the loaves and put them into a floured baguette rack or baking tray.

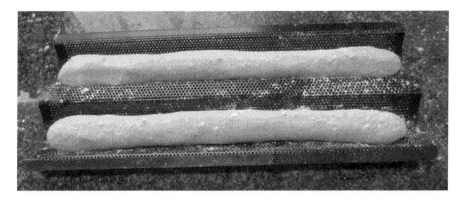

Sprinkle a little flour on top of the baguettes, cover with a tea towel and leave them to prove in a warm place for two to three hours until nearly doubled in size.

Once they have nearly doubled in size slash the loaves diagonally several times:

Put them on the middle shelf of the oven, place 100ml of water into a baking dish in the bottom of the oven to create steam and set the oven to 230°C (190°C fan), 450°F or gas mark 8.

Once the oven has come up to temperature, bake the loaves for 15 minutes, then turn the loaves over to equalize baking and bake for another 10-15 minutes until they are a golden colour.

Turn the oven off and leave the loaves in the cooling oven, with the door slightly open, for a further 5 minutes, then turn out onto a rack to cool.

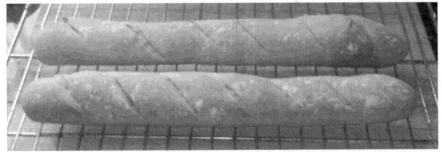

Baked baguettes cooling on rack

Tip: You can also use the better sourdough (sponge method) in place of the basic sourdough method, just use the calculator at the back of the book to adjust the ingredients.

Multi Grain Sourdough

This is another variation on the better sourdough method or you can use the best sourdough method if you have a banneton and cloche.

Ingredients

Flour	200g	strong white bread flour
	200g	multi-grain or mixed seed flour
Water	220ml	preferably filtered water at room temperature
Starter	100ml	sourdough starter at room temperature
Salt	1 teaspoon	preferably sea salt

Method

In the evening, get the sourdough starter out of the fridge and bring it up to room temperature for about 2 hours (it should foam and bubble). Make the sponge by mixing the sourdough starter, water and half the flour but not the salt and leave in a bowl covered with cling-film overnight.

Feed the starter with enough flour and water to replace the starter used, leave it at room temperature for 2 hours and then return it to the fridge.

In the morning the sponge should be fermenting (thick and bubbly). Add the other half of the flour and salt and mix well. Add more flour or water if necessary but keep the dough as sticky as possible.

Turn the dough out onto a lightly floured surface and knead until the dough is smooth and satiny (around 10 minutes).

Shape the dough and put it on a baking sheet, dust with flour, cover with a tea towel and proof in a warm place for two to three hours until nearly doubled in size.

Slash the top of the loaf with a sharp bread knife and put it in on a low shelf in the oven. Put 100ml of water into an ovenproof dish in the bottom of the oven (to create steam) and set the oven to 230°C (190°C fan), 450°F or gas mark 8. Bake for 35 to 40 minutes once the oven has got up to temperature or until the crust is golden, turn the oven off and leave the bread in the cooling oven, with the door slightly open, for another 5 minutes, then turn the loaf out onto a rack to cool for at least an hour.

Sourdough Pizza

This is based on the basic sourdough bread method and will produce two thin crust pizzas.

Ingredients

Flour	350g	strong white bread flour
Water	175ml	preferably filtered water at room temperature
Starter	175ml	sourdough starter at room temperature
Salt	1 teaspoon	preferably sea salt
Oil	1 tablespoon	olive oil

Method

Mix the starter and water in a measuring jug and mix the flour and salt in a large mixing bowl. Rub the olive oil into the flour, then slowly add the water and sourdough starter stirring it until you have added all the liquid and have formed a solid ball of dough. Add a little more flour if it is too runny or a little more water if it is too dry. It should end up as a solid but slightly sticky ball of dough.

Transfer the dough to a lightly floured surface and knead until smooth and easy to handle (around 10 minutes) and form it into a smooth ball.

Return the dough to the mixing bowl, cover with cling film and leave to prove in a warm place for two to four hours until roughly doubled in size.

Gently knock back the dough, divide it into two balls, then flatten them and roll them out and place on lightly-oiled pizza dishes

Leave them to prove in a warm place for two to three hours until doubled in thickness.

Heat the oven to 250°C (fan 200°C), 475°F or gas mark 9 or even hotter.

Spread tomato paste onto the pizza bases and add cheese, basil, anchovies, black olives or any other toppings, drizzle with olive oil and bake for 10 minutes or until golden and serve immediately.

Tip: You can also use the better sourdough method (sponge and single raise) just adjust the ingredients using the calculator at the back of the book.

Sourdough Bagels

This is based on the basic sourdough bread method and will produce four good sized bagels.

Ingredients

Flour	240g	strong white bread flour
Water	120ml	preferably filtered water at room temperature
Starter	120ml	sourdough starter at room temperature
Salt	¾ teaspoon	preferably sea salt
Oil	½ tablespoon	olive oil
Soda	½ tablespoon	baking soda

Method

Mix the starter and water in a measuring jug and mix the flour and salt in a large mixing bowl. Rub the olive oil into the flour, then slowly add the water and sourdough starter stirring it until you have added all the liquid and have formed a solid ball of dough. Add a little more flour if it is too runny or a little more water if it is too dry. It should end up as a solid but slightly sticky ball of dough.

Transfer the dough to a lightly floured surface and knead until smooth and easy to handle (around 10 minutes) and form it into a smooth ball.

Return the dough to the mixing bowl, cover with cling film and leave to prove in a warm place for two to four hours until doubled in size. Put the dough back on a floured surface, divide into four and roll into balls.

Roll the pieces into balls, slightly flatten them and poke your forefinger through the middle to form a hole. Slide your other forefinger into the hole and twirl the dough round to form a ring.

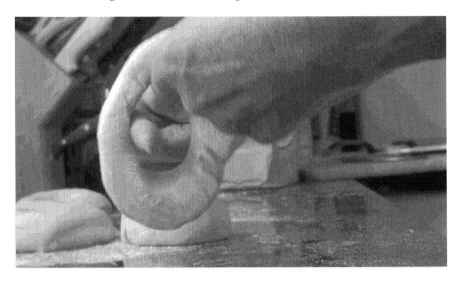

Put the four rings of dough onto a floured baking tray.

Sprinkle with flour, cover with a tea towel and leave to rise for in a warm place for around 2 hours until they are 1½ the size.

Preheat the oven to 220°C (180°C fan), 425°F or gas mark 7 and at the same time fill a large saucepan with water and bring it to the boil.

Once the water is boiling, add the baking soda carefully to the boiling water then, using a slotted spoon, carefully lower a bagel into the boiling water and boil for one minute, then use the spoon to turn it over and boil for another minute on the other side. Again using a slotted spoon, transfer the bagel to the baking sheet and repeat the process for the other three bagels.

Put the baking sheet on the middle shelf of the oven and bake for around 20 minutes until the bagels are golden.

Place on a rack to cool.

Quick Sourdough

If you want to make sourdough bread but don't have the necessary time you can speed the process up by adding some dried yeast. It will impact the flavor somewhat but by also using sourdough starter it will retain some of the sourdough characteristics. This method uses a single raise.

Ingredients

350g strong white flour
175ml sourdough starter
175ml warm water
1tsp dried yeast
1tsp salt

Method

Combine the sourdough starter and warm water in a measuring jug.

Put the flour in a large mixing bowl and mix in the yeast, then stir in the salt.

Add the water and sourdough to the flour, yeast and salt, a little at a time, mixing it in, until a ball of dough is formed.

Transfer the dough to a lightly floured surface and knead until smooth and easy to handle (around 10 minutes).

Shape the loaf as required for a banneton, bread tin or baking tray, sprinkle with flour, cover with a tea towel and leave to prove in a warm place for about an hour until doubled in size.

Slash the top of the loaf with a sharp bread knife and put it in on a low shelf in the oven. Put 100ml of water into an ovenproof dish in the bottom of the oven (to create steam) and set the oven to 230°C (190°C fan), 450°F or gas mark 8. Bake for 35 to 40 minutes once the oven has got up to temperature or until the crust is golden, turn the oven off and leave the bread in the cooling oven, with the door slightly open, for another 5 minutes, then turn the loaf out onto a rack to cool for at least an hour.

Tip: If you have another hour to spare a double rise would improve the sourdough taste. Just follow the basic sourdough method but with an hour for each rise.

Soda Bread

Irish soda bread (arán sóide) can be made using wholemeal, white flour, or a mixture of both. It is made using sodium bicarbonate (baking soda) as the leavening agent instead of yeast. The ingredients are flour, baking soda, salt and buttermilk.

The buttermilk can be replaced by live yoghurt or a mixture of milk and lemon juice, or even Irish stout! The soda begins to act as soon as it comes into contact with the flour and liquid, so the amount of mixing before baking should be minimal and the dough should not be kneaded. It is quick to make (takes under an hour) and is delicious eaten warm from the oven. This is the basic recipe for 'easy-peasy' Irish soda bread:

Ingredients

320g strong wholemeal flour
1 teaspoon bicarbonate of soda
1 teaspoon sea salt
300ml buttermilk, live yoghurt or milk + the juice of half a lemon

Method

Set the oven to 200°C (180°C fan), 400°F or gas mark 6.

While the oven is warming up, mix the flour and bicarbonate of soda in a mixing bowl then stir in the salt. Make a well in the centre and pour in the buttermilk, stirring as you go. It should form a soft dough, not quite sticky. If the mixture is too dry, add a little milk to bring it together.

Tip it out on to a lightly floured surface and work it lightly for about a minute, just long enough to pull it together into a loose ball.

Put the round of dough on a lightly floured baking sheet, flatten it slightly, dust it with flour and mark a deep cross in it with a sharp, serrated knife.

Put it on a low shelf in the oven and bake for 30-35 minutes, until the loaf sounds hollow when tapped underneath.

Put it on a wire rack to cool, but soda bread is best eaten while still warm, spread with salted butter.

CALCULATOR

Metric Calculator

Loaf Size	450g	660g	1000g
Basic Method			
Flour	240g	350g	530g
Water	120ml	175ml	265ml
Starter	120ml	175ml	265ml
Salt	¾ tsp	1 tsp	1½ tsp
Sponge Method			
Flour	270g	400g	600g
Water	150ml	220ml	330ml
Starter	70ml	100ml	150ml
Salt	¾ tsp	1 tsp	1½ tsp

Imperial Calculator

Loaf Size	1 lb	1½ lb	2 lb
Basic Method			
Flour	½ lb	¾ lb	1 lb
Water	4 fl oz	6 fl oz	8 fl oz
Starter	4 fl oz	6 fl oz	8 fl oz
Salt	¾ tsp	1 tsp	1½ tsp
Sponge Method			
Flour	10 oz	14½ oz	19 oz
Water	5 fl oz	7½ fl oz	10 fl oz
Starter	2½ fl oz	3½ fl oz	4¾ fl oz
Salt	¾ tsp	1 tsp	1½ tsp

Notes

The converted imperial values given in the calculator, are the closest approximates to the metric values and not a direct conversion.

As the starter ingredients (flour and water) are both measured by volume (cups) any size cups will work for either system.

LINKS

The following links provide some useful information together with the sale of sourdough starter, flour and baking bits.

Sourdough Home

At sourdoughhome.com for shopping, recipes, tips and techniques.

Bakery Bits

At bakerybits.co.uk for San Francisco sourdough starter and lots of other goodies (including the La Cloche baking dome).

Sourdough Companion

At sourdough.com is a community of bakers (of all levels) interested in the art of naturally risen breads (i.e. bread risen with bacteria and wild yeasts). With recipes, tutorials and discussions.

BBC Food Recipes

At www.bbc.co.uk/food/recipes for lots of recipes for sourdough bread and advice on creating a starter.

Breadtopia

At www.breadtopia.com for lots of recipes and advice on baking sourdough bread.

Tips and Tricks

From the Nourished Kitchen at nourishedkitchen.com/sourdough-tips-and-tricks/ for tips and tricks on working with sourdough.

The Fresh Loaf

At www.thefreshloaf.com for news and information for amateur bakers and artisan bread enthusiasts. They also have some good discussions on the La Cloche and other baking domes and even a link to a way of making one for under $5!

International School of Baking

At www.schoolofbaking.com/sourdough_tips.htm with lots of detailed information on the sourdough process.

Sourdough Primer

At www.kingarthurflour.com for a sourdough primer and sourdough essentials from King Arthur Flour.

Baking Mad

At www.bakingmad.com for sourdough and other baking recipes and tips from Allinson Flour.

Sourdough Adventures

My own blog at sourdougheasy.blogspot.co.uk where I provide some more information on the sourdough experience, updates and feedback.

Or just enter 'sourdough' in your favourite search engine and be rewarded with endless other sources.

The links above were all correct at the time of publication. If any fail to work please let me know via my blog and I'll update them.

About the Author

John Carroll is a former project management consultant who worked in Europe and the United States. He is a Member of the British Computer Society, a Chartered Engineer, European Engineer and has a Masters in Information Technology from the University of Exeter.

Now retired, John lives in the South West of England where, in addition to writing and baking sourdough bread, he enjoys walking, cycling, swimming, wine making and drinking beer at The Bridge Inn, Topsham.

John is also the author of the following books:

Project Management in easy steps
Microsoft Project in easy steps
Project 2000 in easy steps
Project 2002 in easy steps
Project 2007 in easy steps
Project 2010 in easy steps
Project 2013 in easy steps
Effective Project Management in easy steps
Agile Project Management in easy steps
Effective Time Management in easy steps
Project Program and Portfolio Management in easy steps
The Way of the Project Manager

Printed in Great Britain
by Amazon